P9-DHI-975

MONET's
Rivers & Seas
DAY BOOK

MONET's
Rivers & Seas
DAY BOOK

Twilight (Venice)
1908
ISHIBASHI FOUNDATION,
BRIDGESTONE MUSEUM OF ART, TOKYO

EBURY PRESS STATIONERY

FIRST PUBLISHED IN 1992 BY EBURY PRESS STATIONERY
AN IMPRINT OF THE RANDOM CENTURY GROUP
RANDOM CENTURY HOUSE, 20 VAUXHALL BRIDGE ROAD,
LONDON SW1V 2SA
COPYRIGHT © RANDOM CENTURY GROUP 1992

WHILST EVERY EFFORT HAS BEEN MADE TO ENSURE ACCURACY, THE
PUBLISHERS CANNOT ACCEPT LIABILITY FOR ERRORS.

ALL RIGHTS RESERVED. NO PART OF THIS BOOK MAY BE REPRODUCED
IN ANY FORM OR BY ANY MEANS WITHOUT PERMISSION IN WRITING
FROM THE PUBLISHER.

SET IN GOUDY OLD STYLE
BY ✳ TEK-ART LTD., ADDISCOMBE, CROYDON, SURREY

PRINTED IN ITALY
DESIGNED BY DAVID FORDHAM
PICTURE RESEARCH BY MARY JANE GIBSON
EDITED BY CAROLINE TAGGART

ISBN 0 09175 128 4

FRONT COVER ILLUSTRATION: CAP D'ANTIBES, 1888; COURTAULD INSTITUTE GALLERIES, LONDON

BACK COVER ILLUSTRATION: THE BRIDGE AT ARGENTEUIL, 1874; MUSÉE D'ORSAY, PARIS

OPPOSITE ILLUSTRATION: RED BOATS, ARGENTEUIL, 1875; MUSÉE DU LOUVRE, PARIS

PHOTOCREDITS: ARTOTHEK/JOACHIM BLAUEL; BRIDGEMAN ART LIBRARY; COLORPHOTO HINZ; FINE ART PHOTOGRAPHS;
LAUROS/GIRAUDON; STUDIO LOURMEL/PHOTO ROUTHIER; REUNION DES MUSÉES NATIONAUX

Introduction

CLAUDE MONET (1840-1926) unwittingly gave the Impressionist movement its name when critics picked up on the title of a painting he exhibited in 1874: *The Port of Le Havre – Impression: Sunrise.* Certainly his work, with its emphasis on catching impressions of light and atmosphere, is well described by that term. The writer Emile Zola said that Monet seemed to respond almost intuitively to nature, producing 'sketches rapidly brushed for fear of losing the first impression'.

Although born in Paris, Monet spent his childhood and youth at Le Havre, where he met the painter Eugène Boudin, who inspired him to work out of doors and to study the beauties of nature. Throughout the 1860s, the Normandy coast was a favourite subject. Monet's lifelong fascination with light is obvious in these early works. He earned praise for his tonal variation even when, as in *Pointe de la Hève at Low Tide* (1865), the principal colour of the painting was grey. Zola admired the portrayal of dirty, sandy water in *Jetty at Le Havre* (1868), comparing it favourably to the usual 'marine paintings in sugar candy'.

In 1871, Monet moved to Argenteuil, a large village on the Seine. The river at Argenteuil was a favourite haunt of boating enthusiasts, and the sailing boat is a frequent subject in Monet's work during this period, although the preoccupation with light and tone remains. In *The Bridge at Argenteuil* (1874), the interest of the picture lies in the shimmering of the water and the reflection of the boats in it.

After a period at Vétheuil, Monet moved along the Seine to Giverny, where he made the famous waterlily pond that was the subject of his *Nymphéas* series and dominated his work for the last twenty years of his life. He originally portrayed the waterlilies in comparatively realistic landscapes, including the Japanese bridge that was a feature of the garden. But by 1904 the bridge had been eliminated and the surface of the water became the subject of the paintings. Monet's concentration on the areas that absorbed or reflected light have led to him being described as the 'first twentieth century painter' – a forerunner of the abstract movement to come.

The Break Up at Vetheuil,
1883
PRIVATE COLLECTION

January

1

2

3

4

5

6

7

Cap Martin,
1884
PRIVATE COLLECTION

January

8

9

10

11

12

13

14

Waterloo Bridge, Cloudy
Weather,
1900
HUGH LANE MUNICIPAL
GALLERY OF MODERN
ART, DUBLIN

January

15

16

17

18

19

20

21

The Beach at Sainte-
Adresse,
1867
MR & MRS LEWIS LARNED
COBURN MEMORIAL COLL,
CHICAGO ART INSTITUTE

January

22

23

24

25

26

27

Calm Sea,
1881
PRIVATE COLLECTION

28

January

29

30

31

February

1

2

3

Vetheuil in the Fog,
1879
MUSÉE MARMOTTAN

4

February

5

6

7

8

9

10

11

Stormy Sea, Belle Ile,
1886
MUSÉE D'ORSAY, PARIS

February

12

13

14

15

16

17

18

Valley of the Petite
Creuse,
1889
MUSEUM OF FINE ARTS,
BOSTON. (BEQUEST OF
DAVID P. KIMBALL IN
MEMORY OF HIS WIFE,
CLARA BERTRAM
KIMBALL)

February

19

20

21

22

23

24

Pointe de la Hève at
Low Tide,
1865
KIMBELL ART MUSEUM,
FORT WORTH, TEXAS

25

February

26

27

28

29

March

1

2

The Grand Canal,
Venice,
1908
FINE ARTS MUSEUMS OF
SAN FRANCISCO. GIFT OF
OSGOOD HOOKER.

3

March

4

5

6

7

8

9

10

Cap d'Antibes,
1888
COURTAULD INSTITUTE
GALLERIES,
LONDON

March

11

12

13

14

15

16

17

Bridge on the Thames –
Westminster Bridge,
187?
PRIVATE COLLECTION

March

18

19

20

21

22

23

24

Rough Sea, Etretat,
1883
MUSÉE DES BEAUX-ARTS,
LYON

March

25

26

27

28

29

30

31

The Doge's Palace,
Venice,
1908
BROOKLYN MUSEUM, NEW
YORK

April

1

2

3

4

5

6

7

Bridge at Argenteuil,
1874
NEUE PINAKOTHEK,
MUNICH

April

8

9

10

11

12

13

14

The Beach at Etretat,
1883
MUSÉE D'ORSAY, PARIS

April

15

16

17

18

19

20

21

Zaandam, Holland,
1871
MUSÉE D'ORSAY, PARIS

April

22

23

24

25

26

27

28

The Seine at Argenteuil,
1873
MUSÉE D'ORSAY, PARIS

April 29

30

May 1

2

3

4

Bordighera, the
Gardener's House,
1884
PRIVATE COLLECTION

5

May

6

7

8

9

10

11

12

Branch of the Seine at
Giverny,
1897
MUSÉE D'ORSAY, PARIS

May

13

14

15

16

17

18

19

Port Donnant, Belle Ile,
1887
YALE UNIVERSITY ART
GALLERY, GIFT OF MR &
MRS PAUL MELLON, BA
1929

May

20

21

22

23

24

25

26

Regatta at Argenteuil,
1872
MUSÉE D'ORSAY, PARIS

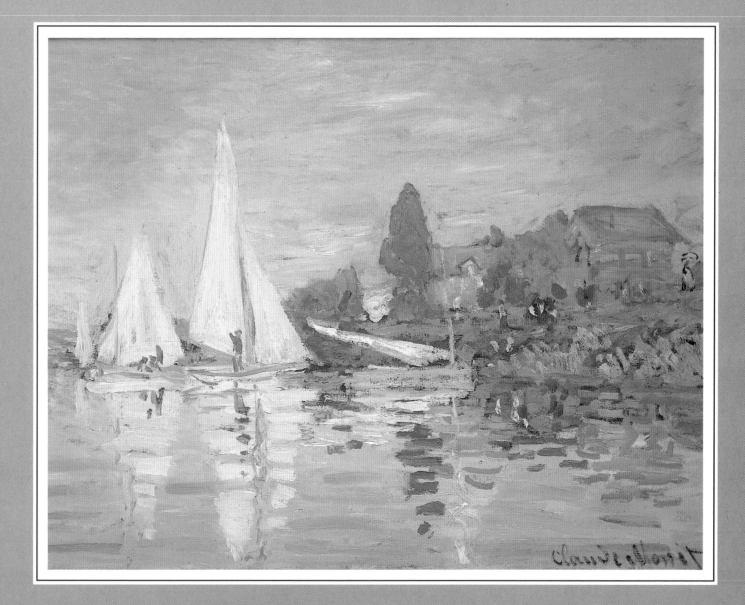

May

27

28

29

30

31

June

1

2

Cliffs at Varengeville,
1882
LEFEVRE GALLERY,
LONDON

June

3

4

5

6

7

8

9

Road at La Cavée,
Pourville,
1882
MUSEUM OF FINE ARTS,
BOSTON. BEQUEST OF MRS
SUSAN MASON LORING

June

10

11

12

13

14

15

16

The Terrace at Sainte-
Adresse,
1866
METROPOLITAN MUSEUM
OF ART, NEW YORK

June

17

18

19

20

21

22

23

The Bridge at
Argenteuil,
1874
MUSÉE D'ORSAY, PARIS

June

24

25

26

27

28

29

30

Ventimiglia,
1884
GLASGOW CITY ART
GALLERY AND MUSEUM

July

1

2

3

4

5

6

Through the Trees,
Ile de la Grande Jatte,
1878
PRIVATE COLLECTION

7

July

8

9

10

11

12

13

14

Cap Martin, near
Menton,
1884
MUSEUM OF FINE ARTS,
BOSTON. JULIANA CHENEY
EDWARDS COLLECTION

July

15

16

17

18

19

20

21

The Blue Boat,
1887
PRIVATE COLLECTION

July

22

23

24

25

26

27

28

Antibes, View from the
Gardens of the Salis,
1888
PRIVATE COLLECTION

July

29

30

31

August

1

2

3

The Seine at Lavacourt,
1880
DALLAS MUSEUM OF ART.
MUNGER FUND

4

August

5

6

7

8

9

10

11

A Bend in the Epte
River, near Giverny,
1888
PHILADELPHIA MUSEUM
OF ART, WILLIAM L.
ELKINS COLLECTION

August

12

13

14

15

16

17

18

The Dock at Argenteuil,
1872
MUSÉE D'ORSAY, PARIS

August

19

20

21

22

23

24

The Blue Sea at
Antibes,
1888
KUNSTMUSEUM, BASEL

25

August

26

27

28

29

30

31

The Banks of the Seine
at Argenteuil,
1872
LEFEVRE GALLERY,
LONDON

September

1

September

2

3

4

5

6

7

8

The Customs House at
Varengeville,
1882
MUSEUM BOYMANS-VAN
BEUNINGEN, ROTTERDAM

September

9

10

11

12

13

14

The Boat at Giverny,
1887
MUSÉE D'ORSAY, PARIS

15

September

16

17

18

19

20

21

22

Pleasure Boats,
Argenteuil,
1872
MUSÉE D'ORSAY, PARIS

September

23

24

25

26

27

28

29

The Railway Bridge at
Argenteuil,
1873/4
MUSÉE D'ORSAY, PARIS

30

1

2

3

4

5

Sailing Boats at Etretat,
1886
PUSHKIN MUSEUM,
MOSCOW

6

October

7

8

9

10

11

12

13

Argenteuil, Early
Evening,
1872
PRIVATE COLLECTION

October

14

15

16

17

18

19

20

Parliament, London
(Patch of Sun in
the Fog),
1904
MUSÉE D'ORSAY, PARIS

October

21

22

23

24

25

26

The Rocks at Belle Ile,
1886
MUSÉE D'ORSAY, PARIS

27

October

28

29

30

31

November

1

Waterloo Bridge,
1903
HERMITAGE MUSEUM,
LENINGRAD

2

3

November

4

5

6

7

8

9

10

The 'Pyramides' at Port-
Coton, Belle-Ile,
1886
NY CARLSBERG
GLYPTOTEK, COPENHAGEN

November

11

12

13

14

15

16

17

Seashore at Fécamp,
1881
PRIVATE COLLECTION

November

18

19

20

21

22

23

Impression, Sunrise,
1872
MUSÉE MARMOTTAN,
PARIS

24

November

25

26

27

28

29

30

December

1

The Lighthouse at
Honfleur,
1864
PRIVATE COLLECTION

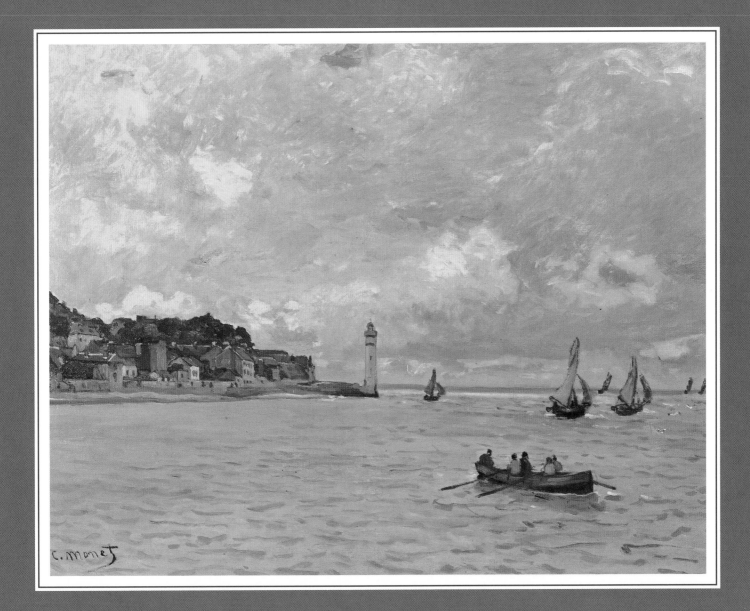

December

2

3

4

5

6

7

8

Houses of Parliament,
London,
1904
MUSÉE DES BEAUX-ARTS,
LILLE

December

9

10

11

12

13

14

Amsterdam,
c. 1874
PRIVATE COLLECTION

15

December

16

17

18

19

20

21

22

Waterloo Bridge,
1902
PRIVATE COLLECTION

December

23

24

25

26

27

28

29

The Break-up of the Ice,
1880
MUSÉE DES BEAUX ARTS,
LILLE

December

30	
31	

Regatta at Argenteuil
MUSEE DU LOUVRE, PARIS